Quiet Moments in Nature

Lessons From the Sky

A 31 Day Journaling Devotional with Discussion Questions

Doris Hoover

Doris Hoover

EABooks Publishing
Your Partner In Publishing

Quiet Moments in Nature, Lessons From the Sky, by Doris Hoover
Copyright @ 2022 Doris Hoover

All rights reserved. No part of this publication may be reproduced or transmitted in any form or by any electronic or mechanical means including photo copying, recording, or any information storage and retrieval system now known or to be invented, without permission in writing from the publisher or the author.

Scripture quotations are taken from the *Holy Bible, New International Version®, NIV®.* Copyright © 1973, 1978, 1984, 2011 by Biblica, Inc.™ used by permission of Zondervan. All rights reserved worldwide. www.zondervan.com. The "NIV and "New International Version" are trademarks registered in the United States Patent and Trademark Office by Biblica, Inc.™

Cover design: Bob Ousnamer
Cover photos by Doris Hoover
Page layout: Robin Black

ISBN: 978-1-955309-13-4

Published by EA Books Publishing, a division of
Living Parables of Central Florida, Inc. a 501c3
EABooksPublishing.com

Dedication

To the Creator of the Sky

Table of Contents

One – Who Am I?... 7
Two – The Language of the Sky........................... 11
Three – A Message in the Wind 15
Four – Sing Your Own Song............................. 19
Five – Dreams, Snowflakes, and Blessings 23
Six – Holy Silence..................................... 27
Seven – Questions 31
Eight – Trusting in the Night Watch.................... 35
Nine – Breaking Free 39
Ten – Specially Designed 43
Eleven – The Day You Were Born....................... 47
Twelve – God's Extraordinary Covenants................ 51
Thirteen – Relief from Summer Heat 55
Fourteen – The Wonder of Snow........................ 59
Fifteen – Light and Shadows 63
Sixteen – Faith and a Song 67

Seventeen – Set Apart.............................. 71
Eighteen – A Cloud Event........................... 75
Nineteen – Heavenly Vision......................... 79
Twenty – Morning Star.............................. 83
Twenty-one – In Praise of God 87
Twenty-two – From Sunrise to Sunset 91
Twenty-three – Like a Weaned Child 95
Twenty-four – The Sound of Grace 99
Twenty-five – Invisible and Visible 103
Twenty-six – A Place of Cool Refreshment 107
Twenty-seven – Transforming Light................. 111
Twenty-eight – Unpredictable...................... 115
Twenty-nine – Snowy Whiteness 119
Thirty – Sunset Reflections....................... 123
Thirty-one – My Story 127

Thou Thinkest Lord of Me

E. D. Mund, Edmund S. Lorenz

Amid the trials which I meet
Amid the thorns that pierce my feet
One tho't remains supremely sweet
Thou thinkest Lord of me

The cares of life come thronging fast
Upon my soul their shadow cast
Their gloom reminds my heart at last
Thou thinkest Lord of me

Let shadows come let shadows go
Let life be bright or dark with woe
I am content for this I know
Thou thinkest Lord of me

Chorus:
Thou thinkest Lord of me
Thou thinkest Lord of me
What need I fear when Thou art near
And thinkest Lord of me

[www.ccli.com CCLI Song # 603255
Words: Public Domain]

One

Who Am I?

*When I consider your heavens, the work of your fingers,
the moon and the stars, which you have set in place,
what is man that you are mindful of him,
the son of man that you care for him?*

Psalm 8:3-4

The Lord displays His majesty in the skies. He tosses silver sequins into the night, creating heavenly dot-to-dot pictures. He staves off total darkness by providing a soft glow from the moon and stars. At dawn, God ignites the horizon with a fiery sunrise. Then at day's end, He sweeps iridescent colors above our heads. "O Lord, our Lord, how majestic is your name in all the earth!" (Psalm 8:9).

David, the shepherd boy who became a king, wrote many of the psalms in the Bible. As he composed Psalm 8, David marveled at God's glorious work in the heavens and wondered how *he* fit in the universe. Maybe, like David, you've wondered about *your* place in this world. Maybe, like me, you've asked, "Who am I to God?"

Two of my grandsons design miniature worlds with small building blocks. When I visit, they pull me into the playroom and say, "Come see what we made, Grandma!" I *ooh* and *ahh* over their creations while they proudly point out the intricate details I overlooked. Their creations are a labor of love. Every detail is significant to them.

If children invest such careful attention to the worlds they create, how much more does our Heavenly Father? When the Lord made us, He paid attention to each detail. "Indeed, the very hairs of your head are all numbered" (Luke 12:7). God even endowed us with some of his own characteristics. "So God created man in his own image" (Genesis 1:27). What can be more special than that?

Although we may be dwarfed by the size of the universe, we are the most significant part of creation. We're intentionally designed in our Father's image. Nothing else in creation has been given that honor.

Only we were given a Savior. God gave His only Son as a sacrifice for our sins so we can spend eternity in heaven with Him.

The awe we feel when we gaze upon a star-filled sky, or the wonder we feel in the presence of a magnificent sunset doesn't come close to the emotion the Lord feels when He gazes upon us. We are the special creation of God's hands, heart, and mind. He delights in every aspect of our being. We are highly valued by our Creator and loved more than we could ever imagine. That's who we are.

*Lord, we're speechless when we truly understand who **we** are to You.*

Personal Reflections

Discussion Questions

1. The Lord thinks of you. How does that thought from the hymn impact you?

2. Describe the most beautiful sky you've ever seen. What does that experience say to you about the Creator of the sky?

3. **Delve deeper:** Read Genesis 1:1-19; Psalm 139:13-18. What do these passages tell you about God and your value to Him?

Joyful Joyful We Adore Thee

Edward Hodges, Henry Van Dyke, Ludwig van Beethoven

Joyful joyful we adore Thee
God of glory Lord of love
Hearts unfold like flow'rs before Thee
Opening to the sun above
Melt the clouds of sin and sadness
Drive the dark of doubt away
Giver of immortal gladness
Fill us with the light of day

All Thy works with joy surround Thee
Earth and heav'n reflect Thy rays
Stars and angels sing around Thee
Center of unbroken praise
Field and forest vale and mountain
Flowery meadow flashing sea
Chanting bird and flowing fountain
Call us to rejoice in Thee

Mortals join the mighty chorus
Which the morning stars began
Father love is reigning o'er us
Brother love binds man to man
Ever singing march we onward
Victors in the midst of strife
Joyful music lifts us sunward
In the triumph song of life

[www.ccli.com CCLI Song #25321 Words: Public Domain]

Two
The Language of the Sky

The heavens declare the glory of God; the skies proclaim the work of his hands. Day after day they pour forth speech; night after night they display knowledge. There is no speech or language where their voice is not heard. Their voice goes out into all the earth, their words to the end of the world.

Psalm 19:1-4

As the sun crept above the horizon, its light beams sparkled on the moist grass. The sun seemed to be saying, "Wake up! Step into the dewy freshness of a new day."

David was inspired to write Psalm 19 while he pondered messages expressed by the sky. He believed the sky's language could be seen and understood by everyone everywhere.

I wonder how many of us listen to the sky's utterances. I decided to challenge myself to interpret this celestial language. I was amazed at the variety of ways in which the sky communicates.

The daytime sky speaks through the color blue, a color that calms the human body and mind. If we listen closely, the heavens soothe and restore our anxious spirits with gentle sighs of peace. A language of slow deep breaths wafts from the eternal blue. *Ahh! God's peace!*

Sometimes the sky speaks with wind, hail, rain, and sleet. The heavens bellow *warnings* of God's power, crying out, "Do not provoke the Lord to anger." It's a language that commands respect. Words of *caution*.

At sunrise and sunset, the sky bursts into joyous song. Its music floats across the horizon in a symphony of color. Crimson, fire orange, pink, and violet banners proclaim, "Glory to God in the highest!" A language of *praise*.

The moon and stars appear as night-lights when the sky turns navy blue. They carry a message of reassurance to calm our fear of darkness. The night sky coos a tender lullaby, "Lie down and sleep in peace; the Lord watches over you." *Comfort* words.

In its unique way, the sky expresses messages of peace, warning, praise, and comfort. The sky's language pleases God.

Our language also pleases God when we speak words of comfort to those in need, when we use words that inspire peace, and when we speak wise words of warning. We join the chorus of the sky when we sing words of adoration for our Lord.

Language is a gift from the Creator. He bestows it upon the sky and us. Let's always be mindful of the words that pass through our lips.

Father, we desire to use our gift of language
to express adoration for You.

Personal Reflections

Discussion Questions

1. According to the hymn, what elements of nature praise God?

2. Discuss ways in which you've experienced the sky's language. What messages have you heard?

3. **Delve deeper:** Read Psalm 119. Besides the sky, what else declares God's goodness?

Holy Ghost With Light Divine

Andrew Reed, Louis Moreau Gottschalk

Holy Ghost with light divine
Shine upon this heart of mine
Chase the gloom of night away
Turn the darkness into day

Holy Ghost with pow'r divine
Cleanse this guilty heart of mine
Long hath sin without control
Held dominion o'er my soul

Holy Ghost with joy divine
Cheer this saddened heart of mine
Bid my many woes depart
Heal my wounded bleeding heart

Holy Spirit all divine
Dwell within this heart of mine
Cast down every idol throne
Reign supreme and reign alone

[www.ccli.com CCLI Song #58460 Words: Public Domain]

Three

A Message in the Wind

He makes winds his messengers.
Psalm 104:4

Whirling air rushes down the street, blustering through trees and lifting leafy branches as though they're billowy skirts. Even though wind is invisible, I can see and feel its effects. As it whips around me, I think about the Lord using the wind to send messages across land and sea.

The Bible refers to the Holy Spirit as wind. Just as we can't see physical wind, we can't see the Holy Spirit, but we can see and feel the effects of Him working in our lives, causing changes in our hearts, attitudes, and circumstances.

Physical wind carries God's messages across land and sea; the Holy Spirit blows them across our souls. The Spirit's message may be as gentle as a breeze when He whispers, *Come to me.*

For many years, I closed my heart to that message. I ignored God's voice and went my own way. Then one day, I actually listened. The Holy Spirit invited me to come to God. When I moved toward the Lord, He welcomed me into His waiting arms.

The Holy Spirit can also carry a message of warning. If we choose to ignore it, the Spirit nips at our conscience the way an icy blast nips at our faces.

There was a time when a certain temptation hounded me. But each time I thought about giving in to it, the Holy Spirit jolted my conscience. I had no peace until I turned away from the temptation and submitted to the Holy Spirit's winds of warning.

In addition to invitations and words of warning, messages of wisdom and guidance come from the Holy Spirit. Even though those messages may drift across our thoughts as lightly as a floating feather, they bring a sense of clarity or assurance that we're making the right decision.

When anxiety overwhelms us, the Spirit calms us with zephyrs of peace. He reminds us the Lord sees and knows our struggles. We can entrust our well being to the Creator of the wind.

The winds of the Spirit move in the deep secret places of each one of us. They may bring a whispered invitation to come to God. They may carry messages of wisdom, guidance, or warning. The Holy Spirit may envelop us with peaceful zephyrs. Whichever message the Lord sends through the winds of the Spirit is a personal message from Him to our hearts. Let's listen carefully because God makes the winds His messengers.

Heavenly Father, open our ears to hear and our hearts to receive the messages You send us through the Holy Spirit.

Personal Reflections

Discussion Questions

1. Read the hymn for this devotion. What actions can the Holy Spirit perform?

2. How has the Holy Spirit interacted with you? How have you responded?

3. **Delve deeper:** Read Psalm 104. The psalmist lists many things God has done. Which is most significant to you? Why?

Have Thine Own Way

Adelaide Addison Pollard, George Coles Stebbins

Have Thine own way Lord
Have Thine own way
Thou art the potter I am the clay
Mold me and make me after Thy will
While I am waiting yielded and still

Have Thine own way Lord
Have Thine own way
Search me and try me Master today
Whiter than snow Lord wash me just now
As in Thy presence humbly I bow

Have Thine own way Lord
Have Thine own way
Wounded and weary help me I pray
Power all power surely is Thine
Touch me and heal me Savior divine

Have Thine own way Lord
Have Thine own way
Hold o'er my being absolute sway
Fill with Thy Spirit till all shall see
Christ only always living in me

[www.ccli.com CCLI Song #28225 Public Domain]

Four
___

Sing Your Own Song

*I know every bird in the mountains,
and the creatures of the field are mine.*
Psalm 50:11

Birds fill the air with music. Goldfinches sing sweet melodies from the thistle. Crows echo endless brassy refrains while chickadees chant *chick-a-dee-dee-dee*. And soaring above all the others, a lone eagle squeals a solo from on high.

God gave each type of bird a unique song. Whether it's a scratchy caw or a melodious trill, each song delights the Lord because it's the very tune God placed within each bird. The birds certainly enjoy singing their God-given songs.

The birds remind me that God also gave me a unique song, and I'm the only one who can sing it. My personality, my abilities, and my physical appearance are all parts of my special song.

A plaque on my wall reads, "Only you can sing your own song." It reminds me to keep the right perspective.

Recently, a close friend shared that when she compared herself to me, she felt lacking. The funny thing is, when I compared myself to her, I felt lacking.

I have another friend whose personality is the opposite of mine. She is decisive and action-oriented. She's out making things happen while I'm sitting on a bench pondering what spiritual lesson I can learn from the birds.

There was a time when I struggled with comparisons. Every time I measured myself against another I felt *less than*. By doing that, I was telling God I didn't value the way He created me.

We were each designed according to God's perfect vision for us. He equipped us with everything we need in order to sing our God-given songs. It's disrespectful to God when we compare ourselves to others and feel lacking. Imagine an eagle wishing it tweeted like a finch or a goldfinch refusing to sing because it couldn't caw like a crow. That may sound absurd, but isn't it just as absurd for us to think our songs, our gifts, and our talents aren't as valuable as those of someone else? The song God gives each of us is unique and can't be compared with any other. We glorify the Lord by using our special qualities to the best of our ability.

If, like me, you've struggled with feeling *less than*, remember, you're the only one who can sing your unique song. It's a gift from the Lord.

Each of us has a song that sounds magnificent to God. He smiles when we sing it with exuberance.

Heavenly Father, thank you for making us the way we are.
We want to glorify You by being the best we can be.
We dedicate our unique songs to You.

Personal Reflections

Discussion Questions

1. This hymn exhorts us to submit to God. What does submission look like? How does the concept of submission connect to today's devotional message?

2. Which special qualities or experiences do you have that help create your unique song? Do you sing your song joyfully? Why or why not?

3. **Delve deeper:** Read Psalm 50. Over what does God have authority? How does that knowledge influence your thoughts about questioning or complaining about the song God gave you to sing? Explain.

Make Me A Blessing

George S. Schuler, Ira Bishop Wilson

Out in the highways and byways of life
Many are weary and sad
Carry the sunshine where darkness is rife
Making the sorrowing glad
Tell the sweet story of Christ and His love
Tell of His pow'r to forgive
Others will trust Him if only you prove
True ev'ry moment you live

Give as 'twas given to you in your need
Love as the Master loved you
Be to the helpless a helper indeed
Unto your mission be true

Chorus:
Make me a blessing make me a blessing
Out of my life may Jesus shine
Make me a blessing O Savior I pray
Make me a blessing to someone today

[www.ccli.com CCLI Song #11603 Words: Public Domain]

Five

Dreams, Snowflakes, and Blessings

In the beginning God created the heavens and the earth.
Genesis 1:1

I watch delicate *ice flowers* drift to the ground in a cascade of frozen rain. Officially, they're called ice crystals or snowflakes, but their magnified appearance is very similar to flowers.

Just as a flower originates from one tiny seed, an ice crystal originates from one frozen droplet of water. As other droplets cling to the core, they form a hexagon and build outward in symmetrical spokes. The end result is a remarkable work of art.

The idea for ice crystals began as God's dream. He envisioned it; then He pursued it. We're blessed with the wonder of snowflakes because the Lord accomplished His dream.

The crystal of a dream stirred my heart when I realized the Lord answers my prayers by teaching me spiritual lessons through nature. That realization became the frozen droplet of a dream. I envisioned writing devotions that inspire others to see how God teaches us through nature.

I applied myself to writing devotions, but I soon realized that having a dream is different from accomplishing it. I had to overcome many obstacles, the greatest being self-doubt. To this day, I struggle with doubt and wonder if my words inspire others.

Finding an outlet for publishing was another challenge. As rejection letters stacked up, my self-doubt increased. I questioned whether I was wasting my time pursuing this dream.

Then I faced dream crushers. A dream is as fragile as a snowflake that can be crushed by a careless touch; likewise, careless remarks can destroy a fragile dream. My dream was almost crushed by thoughtless remarks from others. But I refused to give up. I saw the beauty of my dream and I believed in it. Like frost on a windowpane, my dream was etched on my heart. I chose to protect it. I continue to write devotions, believing they will bring a blessing to others.

We're all dreamers by nature because we were created in the image of God, the greatest dreamer ever. Dreams are blessings from our heavenly Father, so they deserve to be protected. They're worthy of our commitment to pursue them despite the obstacles we encounter.

Are you pursuing the dream God placed in your heart? It's a worthy dream—don't give up on it.

God entrusts us with dreams that are as remarkable as ice crystals. He will help us accomplish them so they'll bring blessings to the world.

Father, help us guard the dreams You place in our hearts.
Give us courage and strength to overcome every obstacle. Lord,
we trust You to make our dreams become blessings.

Personal Reflections

Discussion Questions

1. In what ways does the hymn encourage us to be a blessing to others?

2. Share a dream God placed in your heart. How has it progressed? In what ways do you see your dream bringing a blessing to others?

3. **Delve deeper:** Read Genesis 1. How many dreams does God accomplish in this chapter? Which of His dreams bring special blessings to you?

Holy Holy Holy (Nicaea)

Holy holy holy
Lord God Almighty
Early in the morning
Our song shall rise to Thee
Holy holy holy
Merciful and mighty
God in three persons
Blessed Trinity

Holy holy holy
All the saints adore Thee
Casting down their golden crowns
Around the glassy sea
Cherubim and seraphim
Falling down before Thee
Which wert and art
And evermore shalt be

Holy holy holy
Though the darkness hide Thee
Though the eye of sinful man
Thy glory may not see
Only Thou art holy
There is none beside Thee
Perfect in power
In love and purity

Holy holy holy
Lord God Almighty
All Thy works shall praise Thy name
In earth and sky and sea
Holy holy holy
Merciful and mighty
God in three persons
Blessed Trinity

[www.ccli.com CCLI Song #1156 Public Domain]

Six

Holy Silence

*But the Lord is in his holy temple;
let all the earth be silent before him.*
Habakkuk 2:20

From my porch, I watched the fog drift in and spray paint the air with shades of gray. As a damp wool blanket wrapped the coastline, all sound hushed. Birds stopped singing. Rustling leaves hung perfectly still. My wind chimes ceased their clanging.

Not so in my head where worries clamored relentlessly. Questions bombarded my mind: *What if…? What will happen? What should I do?* I was agitated and tense, anticipating outcomes that may never occur. Worries about my adult children and their varied situations consumed my thoughts. I was carrying weights that didn't seem to burden them yet sucked all the energy from me. I was emotionally exhausted. My prayers had become an endless loop of anxious utterings.

Then a soft whisper interrupted the noise in my head, "Be still and know that I am God" (Psalm 46:10). This clear, simple message reminded me that I had lost my perspective. I was focusing on my troubles. I had forgotten to look up to God. He was still reigning over heaven and earth.

The prophet Habakkuk had a similar experience. He was distraught with worry over the trouble the nation of Israel was facing. In his anxiety, he accused God of being silent. God's reply was that He is in his holy temple and all the earth should be silent before Him. In other words, God told Habakkuk to be silent before *Him*. When the prophet shifted his focus away from his worries, and instead focused on God's majesty, Habakkuk's attitude changed. He realized the Lord was completely aware and in control of the situation. Habakkuk had no power to change or affect the current circumstances of Israel. All power belonged to God.

The concluding verses in the book of Habakkuk show us the prophet's new mindset. Habakkuk prays that even though the worst scenario may happen, "yet I will rejoice in the Lord, I will be joyful in God my Savior." Habakkuk's anxieties were silenced when he trusted God's governance of heaven and earth.

Perhaps you're caught up in the relentless noise of worry over situations out of your control. I encourage you to ask the Lord to interrupt your anxious thoughts. Allow God to quiet your mind. Be still before Him. The Lord is aware of your needs, and He's in control of your situation.

The clamor of worry subsides when we focus on the One who has power to work in each circumstance of our lives. God reigns from His holy temple; let us keep silence before Him.

*Father, when we shift our focus from our worries to You,
our anxiety fades. Help us remain silent in Your holy presence.*

Personal Reflections

Discussion Questions

1. In this hymn, how is reverence for God's holiness expressed?

2. Can you recall a time when you released your anxiety to God and then became still in His presence? Describe how you felt in that moment. How did your thinking change?

3. **Delve deeper:** Read Habakkuk 3. Why do you think Habakkuk felt confident to trust God with his worries? In verses 16, 17, and 18, Habakkuk uses the words *yet* and *though*. How do those words show Habakkuk's faith in God?

O God Our Help In Ages Past (St. Anne)

Isaac Watts, William Croft

O God our help in ages past
Our hope for years to come
Our shelter from the stormy blast
And our eternal home

Under the shadow of Thy throne
Thy saints have dwelt secure
Sufficient is Thine arm alone
And our defense is sure

Before the hills in order stood
Or earth received its frame
From everlasting thou art God
To endless years the same

O God our help in ages past
Our hope for years to come
Be Thou our guard while troubles last
And our eternal home

[www.ccli..com CCLI Song #43152 Words: Public Domain]

Seven

Questions

Where were you when I laid the earth's foundation?
Job 38:4

I wish I could have watched as God created the universe; as heavenly bodies appeared out of the darkness; as sky, water, and land took shape; as living things rose up; and as "the morning stars sang together and all the angels shouted for joy" (Job 38:7).

When I try to imagine the genesis of creation, I recall photos of outer space. They show galaxies and, suspended like an immense marble in midair, a beautiful sphere with blue, white, and aqua swirls— our planet Earth. Who could design and create something so wonderful? Only God.

In the thirty-eighth chapter of Job, God asks Job several questions. *Where were you when I laid the earth's foundation; when I marked off its dimensions; when I laid its footings and cornerstone?* These questions were meant to reprimand Job for thinking he could explain God's mind and purposes.

We all need to consider those questions when life events don't make sense to us. If we attempt to interpret the "why," we may be as misguided as Job. Our finite minds lead us to finite explanations. We can't possibly comprehend God's reasons for allowing or not allowing things to happen in our lives. But we can know that the One who created the universe oversees our lives.

So how does that help us face trials? Rather than asking God *why* certain things happen in our lives, we can ask, "Lord, are you *there*?" The answer is clearly revealed in the heavens above us when we see evidence of God's existence in the millions of stars scattered across the night sky, in the hazy band of light known as the Milky Way Galaxy, and in the eight planets that orbit our solar system. These miracles of the sky affirm that God is there.

Rather than asking God *why* we must face various trials, we can ask, "God are you *with* me?" He reassures us in His own words, "For I am the Lord, your God, who takes hold of your right hand and says to you, Do not fear; I will help you" (Isaiah 41:13). We have a promise from the Creator of heaven and earth. He is with us, and He will help us.

We should ask ourselves the most important question of all— will we entrust ourselves to God's care? We can doubt God's presence and power, or we can place all of our trust in the God who created the universe. What will you choose to do?

Father, thank You for revealing Yourself to us through the things You created. Help us to trust You more and more.

Personal Reflections

Discussion Questions

1. The hymn gives a history lesson. What does it teach about God?

2. Can you recall a time when you questioned God about His plan for your life? What emotions were you feeling at that time? How did you resolve any uncertainties you had about God's plan?

3. **Delve deeper:** Read Isaiah 41:8-13. What reassurance do these verses give us when we're facing trials?

I Need Thee Every Hour

Annie Sherwood Hawks, Robert Lowry

I need Thee every hour
Most gracious Lord
No tender voice like Thine
Can peace afford

I need Thee every hour
Stay Thou near by
Temptations lose their pow'r
When Thou art nigh

I need Thee every hour
In joy or pain
Come quickly and abide
Or life is vain

I need Thee every hour
Most Holy One
O make me Thine indeed
Thou blessed Son

Chorus:
I need Thee O I need Thee
Every hour I need Thee
O bless me now my Savior
I come to Thee

[www.ccli.com CCLI #78811 Public Domain]

Eight

Trusting in the Night Watch

*He will not let your foot slip—he who watches
over you will not slumber.*
Psalm 121:3

I watch the sun cast shadows across the clouds as it slowly lowers its window shades. Cottony tufts turn blue-gray in the darkening sky, yet from the darkness, a single star gleams beside a crescent moon — the Lord's night-light.

This evening's sky brings to mind the words of Psalm 121, one of my favorite psalms. It's comforting to know that God doesn't sleep. When I climb into bed, God stays awake and watches over me. I can rest peacefully knowing the Lord has the night watch.

As a young child, I was afraid of the dark. Before I could fall asleep, my mother had to check in my closet and under my bed for monsters. This was a nightly ritual. Only her promise that no creatures were lurking in the corners of my room gave me the confidence to close my eyes and fall asleep. I trusted my mother to watch over me through the night.

An anxious child trusts her parents to keep her safe, but where does an anxious adult turn for help? "I lift up my eyes to the hills—where does my help come from? My help comes from the Lord, the Maker of heaven and earth" (Psalm 121:1-2).

In Psalm 121, David expressed confidence in God, believing nothing would happen to him while he was in the Lord's care. David trusted God with every aspect of his life. He believed God had the night watch as well as the day watch.

Trust is a powerful concept that requires us to be vulnerable. As adults, we usually try to figure out life on our own. But when issues are too complex for us to handle, we need to trust in Someone greater than ourselves.

There is Someone greater than us, *the Maker of heaven and earth,* and He will help us. But believing God will help requires us to trust in a power we can't see. It's like leaning backwards into the unknown and being certain we'll be caught by capable hands.

The Lord promises to catch us if we're willing to lean into Him. David leaned, and then he wrote, "The Lord will keep you from all harm—he will watch over your life; the Lord will watch over your coming and going both now and forever more" (Psalm 121:7-8).

Will we trust God the way David did? Do we have confidence that God is watching over us?

God's faithfulness twinkles from the sky. With heavenly night-lights, the Lord reminds us we can trust Him. We can sleep peacefully because He's keeping watch.

Father, thank you for watching over us—day and night.

Personal Reflections

Discussion Questions

1. What does the hymn teach about why we need God?

2. Trust increases incrementally. Has your trust in God increased over the years? Explain.

3. **Delve deeper:** Read Psalm 121. How does God help us when we're willing to trust in Him?

He Is Able To Deliver Thee

Walter Augustine Ogden

'Tis the grandest theme thro' the ages rung
'Tis the grandest theme for a mortal tongue
'Tis the grandest theme that the world e'er sung
Our God is able to deliver thee

'Tis the grandest theme in the earth or main
'Tis the grandest theme for a mortal strain
'Tis the grandest theme tell the world again
Our God is able to deliver thee

'Tis the grandest theme let the tidings roll
To the guilty heart to the sinful soul
Look to God in faith He will make thee whole
Our God is able to deliver thee

Chorus:
He is able to deliver thee
He is able to deliver thee
Tho' by sin opprest
Go to Him for rest
Our God is able to deliver thee

[www.ccli.com CCLI Song #85361 Words: Public Domain]

Nine

Breaking Free

*In my anguish I cried to the Lord,
and he answered by setting me free.*
Psalm 118:5

Specks of color flit across my field of vision. I glimpse masterful designs painted on tiny wings—mosaics, stripes and polka dots in shades of orange, black, yellow, blue, and white. Beautiful butterflies flutter unfettered and free.

In contrast, their larvae are wingless, earthbound caterpillars that creep along, awaiting the day they'll fly. Butterflies live two very different lives.

I wonder if God created butterflies to demonstrate the power He has to change lives and to free people from their tethers. Metamorphosis isn't just for butterflies—it's for people too.

The Lord can change the lives of broken, defeated people. He helps those chained to addictions or childhood traumas. He frees those shackled to bitter memories. The Lord helps us crack open the cocoon of wrong thinking so we can break free and begin to live in a new way.

When circumstances knocked me to the ground, I wasted years groveling in bitterness, unable to rise above the resentment that kept me in the muck. But Jesus helped me fly above my bitter thoughts by teaching me how to forgive.

It wasn't easy to change the way my mind thought and the way my heart felt. The change required God's power working in me. The Lord helped me see that, by crawling in the dirt of resentment, I was living a caterpillar life

During a period of prayer and self-examination, I wrestled with the pride I used to justify my bitterness. Eventually, the moment of decision came. I had to decide whether I wanted to remain shackled to my resentment or to break free by forgiving the one who hurt me.

Just as a butterfly has to fight its way out of a cocoon, I had to fight my way out of bitterness. But God gave me the power to do it. The act of forgiveness cracked open my cocoon and set me free!

The Lord wants each of us to fly. He didn't create us to crawl through life, dragged down by weights we shouldn't carry. With God's help, we can release the resentments and disappointments that keep us bound. The act of forgiveness helps us break free.

God works in us to bring about change. It's a process, but when our hearts change, so do our thoughts and attitudes. When we're ready to emerge as a new creature, the Lord paints masterful designs in our spirits. They symbolize our stories of overcoming, forgiving, and breaking free. The Lord gives us beautiful victory wings. Then He lifts us in His hand and tells us to fly.

Thank you, Lord, for helping us break free
and for giving us wings to fly.

Personal Reflections

Discussion Questions

1. From what does the hymn tell us we can be delivered?

2. Do you consider yourself to be in the caterpillar or butterfly phase? From what are you struggling to be free? From what have you been set free?

3. **Delve deeper:** Read Psalm 118:5-21. How does the psalmist react to his troubles?

I'll Go Where You Want Me to Go

Carrie E. Rounsefell, Charles Edward Prior, Mary Brown

It may not be on the mountain's height
Or over the stormy sea
It may not be at the battle's front
My Lord will have need of me
But if by a still small voice He calls
To paths I do not know
I'll answer dear Lord
With my hand in Thine
I'll go where You want me to go

Perhaps today there are loving words
Which Jesus would have me speak
There may be now in the paths of sin
Some wanderer whom I should seek
O Savior if Thou wilt be my Guide
Though dark and rugged the way
My voice shall echo
The message sweet
I'll say what You want me to say

Chorus:
I'll go where You want me to go dear Lord
Over mountain or plain or sea
I'll say what You want me to say dear Lord
I'll be what You want me to be

[www.ccli.com CCLI Song #47282 Public Domain]

Ten

Specially Designed

*For we are God's workmanship,
created in Christ Jesus to do good works,
which God prepared in advance for us to do.*
Ephesians 2:10

The moon glows softly in the pre-dawn sky. Standing beneath its serene light, I feel a sense of peace.

Along the eastern horizon, however, another scenario unfolds. Preparing for a grand appearance, the sun rummages through her closet, tossing long colorful scarves across the sky. Finally, choosing a golden outfit, she steps forth and lights up the world.

The Lord created the sun and moon to be very different. The moon gives subtle light to the night sky, but the sun illuminates the day with such intensity the moon fades in the sun's brilliance.

God created these celestial bodies for unique purposes. Similarly, He designed our personalities for unique purposes. We may have traits that resemble the sun or the moon.

Sun people shine in large settings. They have personalities that not only draw attention but also seek attention. When sun people are in a room, everyone knows it. They have a charisma that attracts an audience. Sun people don't fade into the background.

Moon people may pale in the presence of sun people, yet in their own realm, moon people emit a special glow. They bring a sense of tranquility to those around them. Their gifts shine best in intimate settings. Those who know moon people appreciate their quiet ways.

Whether we have a moon or a sun personality, God has work for us that requires us to be exactly who He created us to be. Sun people may impact a greater realm of individuals because their natures shine in big spaces. Christian entertainers and famous evangelists have the ability to share the gospel in large arenas. The Lord created people like them to carry out his work before a huge audience.

But there's also work that needs people whose personalities glow in smaller settings. Consider the woman who visits her lonely neighbor. She may be sharing intimate conversation and a cup of tea with only one person, but she's doing the work God prepared for her to do. She was specially designed for such a task.

The next time we marvel at the gifts and talents we see in others, let's think about the sun and the moon. Each was designed with the exact qualities necessary for them to accomplish God's purpose. We, too, were specially designed to accomplish the work God purposed for us. Whether we shine with intensity or glow softly, we are God's workmanship, created to do good works in His name.

Father, thank you for giving us unique personalities.
May we use them to glorify You.

Personal Reflections

Discussion Questions

1. According to the hymn, how does a submissive servant of God act?

2. Do you consider yourself to have sun or moon traits? Why? How is the Lord leading you to use your special qualities?

3. **Delve deeper:** Read Ephesians 2:1-10. Despite our unique personality traits, what do all believers have in common? How does that influence your thinking about people's differences?

Let Jesus Come Into Your Heart

Lelia Naylor Morris

If you are tired
Of the load of your sin
Let Jesus come into your heart
If you desire a new life to begin
Let Jesus come into your heart

If 'tis for purity now that you sigh
Let Jesus come into your heart
Fountains for cleansing
Are flowing near by
Let Jesus come into your heart

If there's a tempest
Your voice cannot still
Let Jesus come into your heart
If there's a void
This world never can fill
Let Jesus come into your heart

If you would join the glad songs
Of the blest
Let Jesus come into your heart
If you would enter
The mansions of rest
Let Jesus come into your heart

Chorus:
Just now your doubtings give o'er
Just now reject Him no more
Just now throw open the door
Let Jesus come into your heart

[www.ccli.com CCLI Song #98523 Public Domain]

Eleven

The Day You Were Born

You are my Son; today I have become your Father.
Psalm 2:7

I look toward the east where glowing fingers stretch along the horizon. In their glow, clouds turn from gray to pink to neon orange. Suddenly, a brilliant sphere pushes through the clouds and rises above the trees. I watch in awe as a new day is born.

I remember the day my first child was born. As I held this brand new person, only minutes old, my heart whispered, "You're my daughter; today I've become your mother."

From the moment of her birth, *I* became *us*; our lives were intertwined. My daughter relied upon me to satisfy her every need. During those first few months, I learned about the exhausting responsibility of parenthood. But each time I gazed at her, I felt the pure joy of motherhood.

Over time, I gave birth to two more daughters who also filled my heart with wonderment and delight. Eventually, all of my daughters became mothers. They learned the great responsibility of caring for children. Although mothers can satisfy the physical needs of their children, only God can satisfy their spiritual needs.

I was an adult when I became aware of a spiritual longing in my heart. I tried to fill it in different ways: I kept busy; I indulged my pleasures; I sought fulfillment in other people. Nevertheless, nothing could satisfy the yearning in my soul.

I thought religion could fill my longing, so I explored various religious groups. The denomination of my childhood proved to be unsatisfying, as did eastern religions I investigated. An encounter with a New Age group unnerved me when they told me I was living in a state of glee.

All of those dead-end paths prepared me to recognize the true path when I finally found it. I started attending a Christian church that taught the Bible. As I studied God's word, I read about new birth. "I tell you the truth, no one can see the kingdom of God unless he is born again" (John 3:3). "We were therefore buried with him through baptism into death in order that, just as Christ was raised from the dead through the glory of the Father, we too may live a new life" (Romans 6:4).

I chose to follow the example in the Bible. I was buried in the water of baptism and raised to a new life. I was born again as God's child. The longing in my soul was finally satisfied!

The Lord rejoices over our physical birth, but His joy is even greater at our spiritual re-birth. The angels rejoice on the day the Lord proclaims, *You are my child; today I have become your Father.*

Lord, we come to You to be born again.

Personal Reflections

Discussion Questions

1. According to the hymn, how do our lives change when we invite Jesus into our hearts?

2. Have you experienced spiritual rebirth? Will you share your story of that moment? If you haven't been reborn, what's holding you back?

3. **Delve deeper:** Read Psalm 24. Over what does God have authority? Who may enter His presence? What happens when we willingly open the gate of our hearts?

Standing On The Promises

Russell Kelso Carter

Standing on the promises of Christ my King
Through eternal ages let His praises ring
Glory in the highest I will shout and sing
Standing on the promises of God

Standing on the promises that cannot fail
When the howling storms of doubt and fear assail
By the living Word of God I shall prevail
Standing on the promises of God

Standing on the promises I now can see
Perfect present cleansing in the blood for me
Standing in the liberty where Christ makes free
Standing on the promises of God

Standing on the promises I cannot fall
List'ning ev'ry moment to the Spirit's call
Resting in my Savior as my All in All
Standing on the promises of God

Chorus:
Standing standing
Standing on the promises of God my Savior
Standing standing
I'm standing on the promises of God

[www.ccli.com CCLI Song #31803 Public Domain]

Twelve

God's Extraordinary Covenants

*I have set my rainbow in the clouds, and it will be the
sign of the covenant between me and the earth.*
Genesis 9:13

A heavy fleece of clouds dripped for most of the day. Eventually, the clouds dissipated and the sun took their place. But one cloud remained. As it sprinkled water through the sunbeams, a rainbow arced across the sky.

There's nothing quite as spectacular as a rainbow. It's an extraordinary symbol designed by God, a heavenly declaration of His covenant with the earth. God speaks in rainbows!

A covenant is a binding contract. It's a promise, a cross my heart, a pinky swear. It's a vow that can't be broken. When people enter into a contract, they sign in black ink on the dotted line. Sometimes a notary embosses a seal on the paper. A contractual agreement is a significant event carried out in black and white.

God's covenants, however, aren't black and white events—they're multicolored and spectacular! The Lord repeatedly displays His rainbow promise in the sky.

The Lord established other covenants in exceptional ways also. His covenant with the nation of Israel was known as The Law. It was the standard by which the people were to conduct their lives. God would judge them according to the precepts of the Law.

The covenant of The Law was given on Mt. Sinai when Moses met with God. The Lord descended in a cloud while thunder rumbled and lightning flashed. That covenant wasn't written on paper with ink—it was inscribed on stone tablets by God's own hand.

God's covenant with the world was stained red with the blood of Jesus. This is the covenant of redemption for all mankind. The sacrifice of Jesus on the cross made the way for each of us to be forgiven of our sins. That one event has been retold throughout the world for centuries. It's commemorated by Christians each time we eat and drink the Communion.

The covenant that promises eternal life with God in heaven is much more than ink and paper. God sealed this covenant with a living part of Himself. "Having believed, you were marked in him with a seal, the promised Holy Spirit, who is a deposit guaranteeing our inheritance until the redemption of those who are God's possession—to the praise of his glory" (Ephesians 1:13-14).

God uses extraordinary, momentous events to establish His covenants. The terms of His contracts and promises are clearly revealed in the inspired, God-breathed, living words of the Bible. We can stand on the promises God makes in His extraordinary covenants.

Lord, we count on Your promises. May we always show reverence for Your sacred covenants.

Personal Reflections

Discussion Questions

1. According to the hymn, how do God's promises benefit us?

2. In what ways have you acknowledged important events in your life? Symbols, celebrations, covenants?

3. **Delve deeper:** Read Genesis 9:9-17. Why did God create the rainbow? How should we respond to rainbows? Would you consider them to be sacred? Explain.

Dear Refuge Of My Weary Soul

Anne Steele

Dear refuge of my weary soul
On Thee when sorrows rise
On thee when waves of trouble roll
My fainting hope relies
To Thee I tell each rising grief
For Thou alone canst heal
Thy Word can bring a sweet relief
For every pain I feel

But oh when gloomy doubts prevail
I fear to call Thee mine
The springs of comfort seem to fail
And all my hopes decline
Yet gracious God where shall I flee
Thou art my only trust
And still my soul would cleave to Thee
Though prostrate in the dust

Thy mercy seat is open still
Here let my soul retreat
With humble hope attend Thy will
And wait beneath Thy feet
Thy mercy seat is open still
Here let my soul retreat
With humble hope attend Thy will
And wait beneath Thy feet

[www.ccli.com CCLI Song #6258906 Public Domain]

Thirteen

Relief from Summer Heat

I was overcome by trouble and sorrow. Then I called on the name of the Lord: "O Lord, save me!"
Psalm 116:3-4

A cool breeze brings refreshment in hot weather. Low-hanging clouds also provide relief by buffering the sun's intensity. When humidity closes in, the Lord squeezes the clouds like a sponge to release moisture from the air. And in the evening, cooler temperatures make the hot season more bearable. Each weather gift brings welcome relief from summer heat.

At times, our lives have seasons of summer heat when trials bear down on us and there seems to be no relief from our intense problems. But just as God provides refreshment during uncomfortable weather, He provides refreshment during uncomfortable circumstances.

After my father passed away, my sister and I went through a difficult time. Even though it happened in winter, we felt like we were in the middle of a summer heat wave of problems. There were so many loose ends to tie up we didn't know where to begin. Each morning we'd meet at my father's house, sit at the table, and stare blankly ahead of us. The details of what had to be done overwhelmed us. Not knowing where to begin, we asked God to help us.

Like a cooling breeze, the Holy Spirit moved through our circumstances in ways we couldn't have predicted. A friend of a friend knew a person who would adopt our father's dog. A realtor guided us through a complicated house sale. We found suitable accommodations for our brother who needed a place to live.

At times, the Lord acted like a thick cloud shielding us from creditors and real estate turmoil. When we felt completely overwhelmed, the Lord whispered, *I hear your cries for help. Rest in me.* His voice wafted over us like a welcomed breeze. God provided relief from the heat of our troubles.

The same God who refreshes us during the hot days of summer, helps us when life gets hot. He acts as a buffer from the intensity of our trials. Like a cool breeze, the Holy Spirit moves through our circumstances with unexpected solutions.

On summer days, when refreshing breezes cool our skin, we can remember the One who brings cooling relief into our lives. We're not overcome by the heat of trials because the Lord hears our cries and helps us. "I love the Lord, for he heard my voice; he heard my cry for mercy. Because he turned his ear to me, I will call on him as long as I live." (Psalm 116:1-2).

Lord, thank you for hearing our voices
and always bringing relief.

Personal Reflections

Discussion Questions

1. The hymn contrasts taking refuge in God with not going to Him for relief. How do the results of each choice differ?

2. How has God refreshed you during a trial?

3. **Delve deeper:** Read Psalm 116. How did God refresh the psalmist during his difficult times?

Come Thou Fount Of Every Blessing (Nettleton)

John Wyeth, Robert Robinson

Come Thou fount of ev'ry blessing
Tune my heart to sing Thy grace
Streams of mercy never ceasing
Call for songs of loudest praise
Teach me some melodious sonnet
Sung by flaming tongues above
Praise the mount I'm fixed upon it
Mount of Thy redeeming love

Here I raise my Ebenezer
Hither by Thy help I'm come
And I hope by Thy good pleasure
Safely to arrive at home
Jesus sought me when a stranger
Wand'ring from the fold of God
He to rescue me from danger
Interposed His precious blood

O to grace how great a debtor
Daily I'm constrained to be
Let Thy grace Lord like a fetter
Bind my wand'ring heart to Thee
Prone to wander Lord I feel it
Prone to leave the God I love
Here's my heart Lord take and seal it
Seal it for Thy courts above

[www.ccli.com CCLI Song #108389 Public Domain]

Fourteen

The Wonder of Snow

*Does the snow of Lebanon ever vanish from
its rocky slopes? Do its cool waters
from distant sources ever cease to flow?*
Jeremiah 18:14

I love to tilt my head toward the sky while snow sprinkles my face and eyelashes. I'm transfixed by the continuous downflow of tiny wafer-like flakes. Snow fills me with a sense of delight. I'm mesmerized by its unique qualities and its frozen beauty.

Snow benefits the earth and its creatures. In extremely cold regions, it insulates the ground. Without a blanket of snow, plants and roots can't survive frigid temperatures. Snow's insulating properties also shelter animals who live in cold open areas. They can burrow in a snow mound to stay warm. Small creatures use snow as a hiding place from predators.

Snow is also a great reflector. Sun reflects off snow-covered surfaces and warms the surrounding air during daylight hours. And as snow melts, it replenishes the earth with water.

When I think about the qualities of snow, I see a spiritual application. The Lord becomes a blanket of comfort and warmth for us. He wraps us with love so we never feel like we've been left out in the cold. When life seems harsh, we can curl up in the arms of God.

The Lord is also our hiding place and our shelter. We never have to fend for ourselves in inhospitable conditions. "I will take refuge in the shadow of your wings until the disaster has passed" (Psalm 57:1).

The Lord's light reflects warmth into our lives the way sunlight reflects off snow to warm the air. And just as streams of melted snow replenish the earth, the Lord continually replenishes our hearts with streams of love, joy, peace, and hope.

When people forget the wonder of God, it breaks His heart. Today's Scripture addresses such a situation. The nation of Israel lost its enchantment with God and began to worship idols. He reminded them they could count on Him the way they count on snow capping the mountains of Lebanon. God reminded them He's as reliable as cool waters that never cease to flow from the mountains. "Yet my people have forgotten me" (Jeremiah 18:15). "How I have been grieved by their adulterous hearts, which have turned away from me, and by their eyes, which have lusted after their idols" (Ezekiel 6:9). God's children forgot the source of their blessings.

May we always tilt our faces toward the One who blesses us, and may we never forget His faithful provision. Like a child in snow, may we continually be awestruck by the wonder of God.

Lord, You are the wonder of snow and the fount of every blessing. We stand in awe of You.

Personal Reflections

Discussion Questions

1. According to the hymn, why should we be in awe of God? How can we demonstrate our awe for God?

2. Has God been like snow to you? Explain.

3. **Delve deeper:** Read Jeremiah 18:1-12. What does this passage teach about God's right to direct our lives? Knowing that, how should we respond to the Lord?

Nothing Between

Charles Albert Tindley

Nothing between my soul and my Savior
Naught of this world's delusive dream
I have renounced all sinful pleasure
Jesus is mine there's nothing between

Nothing between like worldly pleasure
Habits of life though harmless they seem
Must not my heart from Him ever sever
He is my all there's nothing between

Nothing between my soul and the Savior
So that His blessed face may be seen
Nothing preventing the least of His favor
Keep the way clear keep the way clear
Nothing between my soul and the King

[www.ccli.com CCLI Song #6052030 Public Domain]

Fifteen

Light and Shadows

God is light; in him there is no darkness at all.
I John 1:5

Palm fronds extended long narrow fingers that blocked the sun. They made shadows on the grass, creating a patchwork of light and dark. As I observed the shadows on the grass, I thought of how God shines into my life; yet I often create shadows that block His light.

We create shadows when distractions stand between us and our source of light. Daily chores, exercise, leisure activities, and even volunteer commitments can take up so much of our day there's not much time left to spend in the light of God's word and presence.

The Lord desires to spend time with us. He's delighted when we choose to be with Him. But spending time with God requires effort and a decision on our part.

Mary made such a decision when Jesus visited her home. She sat at his feet, pondering each word the Lord spoke. His light shone directly on her.

Her sister Martha made a different decision. Food preparation was her priority. Because there were people to feed, it was an important chore, but it wasn't the best use of her time. Jesus told Martha, "You are worried and upset about many things, but only one thing is needed. Mary has chosen what is better, and it will not be taken away from her" (Lk.10:41-42).

Even though many of our distractions are important activities, they're not the best use of our time if choosing them means neglecting time with God. Martha created a shadow when food preparation kept her in the kitchen. Her busyness made a shadow between her and the light shining from her living room. She missed the blessing of being in the Lord's presence.

Our Heavenly Father wants us to sit with Him, to sing to Him, to share our thoughts and concerns, and to simply enjoy being in His company.

So how can we remove our self-created shadows? We can prioritize our schedules to include daily, uninterrupted time with the Lord. We can keep God in the forefront of our thoughts by conversing with Him throughout the day and inviting Him to accompany us all day long. And we can look for lessons God teaches through nature, like the lesson we learn from shadows and light.

The Lord waits for us to step out from the shadows so He can bless us with the light of His presence. He waits for us to choose the "better."

Father, we're sorry for allowing distractions to create shadows between us and You. Help us choose wisely so we always stay in Your light.

Personal Reflections

Discussion Questions

1. What does the hymn mention that can come between us and the Lord?

2. Is there one particular thing in your life that's creating a shadow between you and the Lord? What must you do to step out of the shadow? Are you willing to do what it takes?

3. **Delve deeper:** Read 1 John 1:5-10. How can shadows cause a spiritual problem in our lives? How should we respond to the shadows we discover? What may cause us to choose to remain in the shadows?

He Keeps Me Singing (My Heart A Melody)

Luther Burgess Bridgers

There's within my heart a melody
Jesus whispers sweet and low
Fear not I am with thee peace be still
In all of life's ebb and flow

All my life was wrecked by sin and strife
Discord filled my heart with pain
Jesus swept across the broken strings
Stirred the slumb'ring chords again

Feasting on the riches of His grace
Resting 'neath His sheltering wing
Always looking on His smiling face
That is why I shout and sing

Chorus:
Jesus Jesus Jesus
Sweetest name I know
Fills my ev'ry longing
Keeps me singing as I go

[www.ccli.com CCLI Song #27855 Words: Public Domain]

Sixteen

Faith and a Song

My heart is steadfast, O God, my heart is steadfast;
I will sing and make music.
Psalm 57:7

Thick clouds hang from today's sky, yet despite the gray atmosphere, birds sing from the trees. Their cheerful music floats in the air around me. My own clouds hang over me, and the last thing I feel like doing is singing.

In Psalm 57, we read of a heavy cloud that hung over David—King Saul's relentless attempt to kill him. Yet while hiding in a dark cave, fearing for his life, David was confident God would help him. "I will take refuge in the shadow of your wings until the disaster has passed" (Psalm 57:1). David's faith in God was certain. Even in the midst of danger, he could say, "My heart is steadfast, O God, my heart is steadfast; I will sing and make music" (Psalm 57:7).

When I was a little girl, I had an unwavering faith in my daddy. I'd run to him with tears in my eyes and tell him my troubles. Daddy would assure me that everything would be okay, and I believed him with all of my heart. Then, before my tears completely dried, I'd skip away smiling and singing.

Now, as an adult, when troubles come, I run to my heavenly Father. I try to have the childlike faith I had in my daddy, but sometimes my faith is weak. Rather than skipping away with a song and a smile, I walk away with doubts. But even though *I* may have doubts, *the Lord* is faithful.

On this particular day, God used an event in nature to remind me I could trust Him. He sent sunbeams that burst through the clouds and formed a shimmering fan of light. It was a beautiful sky message from the Lord to assure me light would shine through my clouds and everything would be okay. I felt a song rise in my heart.

When we run teary-eyed to our Abba Daddy, He scoops us into His arms and tells us we'll be okay. No trial is too big and no problem is too insignificant for the Lord. He cares about every situation we face, and He shows it in special ways. God usually responds to me through nature. He'll respond to you in a way that's meaningful to you. The Lord always finds a unique way to prove His faithfulness. Each time He does, our faith increases a little more. Perhaps one day our faith will be as steadfast as David's so that, despite our trials, we can sing.

Father, You are always faithful. We want to honor You with greater faith and a song.

Personal Reflections

Discussion Questions

1. According to the hymn, why should we sing?

2. When facing a trial, what is your most common reaction? Does it result in singing?

3. **Delve deeper:** Read Psalm 57. David's trials were severe. Why do you think his faith was steadfast?

Take My Life And Let It Be

Frances Ridley Havergal, Henri Abraham Cesar Malan

Take my life and let it be
Consecrated Lord to Thee
Take my moments and my days
Let them flow in endless praise

Take my hands and make them move
At the impulse of Thy love
Take my feet and let them be
Swift and beautiful for Thee

Take my voice and let me sing
Always only for my King
Take my lips and let them be
Filled with messages from Thee

Take my will and make it Thine
It shall be no longer mine
Take my heart it is Thine own
It shall be Thy royal throne

Take my love my Lord I pour
At thy feet its treasure store
Take myself and I will be
Ever only all for Thee
Amen

[www.ccli.com CCLI Song #1390 Words: Public Domain]

Seventeen

Set Apart

*Know that the Lord has set apart the godly for himself;
the Lord will hear when I call to him.*
Psalm 4:3

Leaning against a sun-warmed boulder, I gaze at clouds floating across a dazzling blue sky. Above the highest cloud, an eagle soars. It flies alone, set apart from other birds—the way God intended.

God also sets apart people and nations. He chose the nation of Israel to be the recipient of the Law, a unique set of moral, social, and spiritual standards. "Out of all the peoples on the face of the earth, the Lord has chosen you to be his treasured possession" (Deuteronomy 14:2). The Law would distinguish Israel as belonging to God.

Christians are also set apart for God. "Once you were not a people, but now you are the people of God; once you had not received mercy, but now you have received mercy (1 Peter 2:10). "'Therefore come out from them and be separate,' says the Lord" (2 Corinthians 6:17).

By definition, *set apart* means to be different or distinguished in some way. The eagle's ability to soar sets it apart from other birds. The Law distinguishes Israel from other nations. As Christians, the choices we make set us apart from the world.

When we choose to adhere to holy values in an unholy world, we distinguish ourselves from others. But people don't always like our choices, nor do they understand why we choose to live differently.

My friend Ann chose to follow a path of longsuffering. Her friends and family didn't understand why she wouldn't leave her cruel husband. Ann persevered through the hurt because she believed the Lord wanted her to stay in her marriage. Her love for the Savior was so strong she willingly followed His example of loving the unlovable. Ann chose to follow a set of values that were different from those around her. The world values pride and retribution; Ann practiced humility and grace. As she strived to imitate the Lord, He comforted her, strengthened her, and lifted her up.

Perhaps you're suffering for choosing to follow God's way. Maybe family or friends criticize your decisions and pull away from you. Being set apart for God isn't always easy.

When the Lord sets us apart, He asks us to live our lives with a distinct set of values; however, when we suffer for our obedience, God doesn't leave us alone. He stays beside us. He gives us courage and strength to follow His ways. When God sets us apart, He lifts us high so we can soar close to Him.

Thank you, Lord, for setting us apart for Yourself.
Help us make choices worthy of such an honor.

Personal Reflections

Discussion Questions

1. The hymn lists ways to be set apart for God. What is our part in being set apart?

2. Have you faced challenges while trying to be set apart for God? Explain.

3. **Delve deeper:** Read Psalm 4. List both the challenges and blessings encountered by those who are set apart for the Lord.

When the Roll Is Called Up Yonder

James Milton Black

When the trumpet of the Lord shall sound
And time shall be no more
And the morning breaks eternal bright and fair
When the saved of earth
Shall gather over on the other shore
And the roll is called up yonder
I'll be there

On that bright and cloudless morning
When the dead in Christ shall rise
And the glory of his resurrection share
When his chosen ones shall gather
To their home beyond the skies
And the roll is called up yonder
I'll be there

Let us labor for the Master
From the dawn till setting sun
Let us talk of all his wondrous love and care
Then when all of life is over
And our work on earth is done
And the roll is called up yonder
I'll be there

Chorus:
When the roll is called up yonder
When the roll is called up yonder
When the roll is called up yonder
When the roll is called up yonder
I'll be there

[www.ccli.com CCLI Song #31315 Words: Public Domain]

Eighteen

A Cloud Event

*Look, he is coming with the clouds,
and every eye will see him.*
Revelation 1:7

Air currents drag their fingers through the clouds forming and re-forming vaporous images, creating works of art on a sky-sized canvas.

The God who grants artistic talent to people also bestows artistic capabilities upon elements of nature. Wind and clouds work together to create masterpieces in the sky. All day, every day, they sculpt vaporous images that stir our imaginations and remind us there's a Master Artist at work. Images continually morph into new images, producing an ongoing show in the clouds.

My mother and I used to recline on a blanket in our backyard to look at the clouds. I would see one image, and she would point out another. The heavenly art show drew our attention away from our daily activities.

Cloud imagery draws our attention to a realm above us, to a place called heaven where God and angels dwell. And we have an open invitation to claim a place in that realm.

In order to claim a seat at an earthly show, we need to buy a ticket. If someone buys it for us, we have to claim it at the Will Call desk or else we're denied entrance to the show.

God purchased our tickets to heaven, but if we don't claim them, we'll be denied entrance to heaven. Our Will Call is the simple act of bowing to the King of Heaven and receiving Him as our Savior. When we do this, God marks our tickets as claimed.

Assured of a place in heaven, we eagerly await the show of shows, the grand finale, when King Jesus appears in the clouds to gather all who belong to Him. "For the Lord himself will come down from heaven, with a loud command, with the voice of the archangel and with the trumpet call of God, and the dead in Christ will rise first. After that, we who are still alive and are left will be caught up together with them in the clouds to meet the Lord in the air. And so we will be with the Lord forever" (1 Thessalonians 4:16-17).

The entire world will witness this event. Some people will rejoice, but others will tremble because they never collected their ticket to heaven. Do you have yours? Why wait?

Lord Jesus, we receive You as our Savior.

Personal Reflections

Discussion Questions

1. The hymn describes the heavenly roll call. What will it be like? Will your name be called?

2. Have you experienced a memorable cloud event? Try to describe it and explain its significance to you.

3. **Delve deeper:** Read 1 Thessalonians 4:13 – 5:6. How does the Apostle Paul describe roll call both before and during the event?

Turn Your Eyes Upon Jesus

Helen H. Lemmel

O soul are you weary and troubled
No light in the darkness you see
There's light for a look at the Savior
And life more abundant and free

Through death into life everlasting
He passed and we follow Him there
Over us sin no more has dominion
For more than conquerors we are

His Word shall not fail you He promised
Believe Him and all will be well
Then go to a world that is dying
His perfect salvation to tell

Chorus:
Turn your eyes upon Jesus
Look full in His wonderful face
And the things of earth
Will grow strangely dim
In the light of His glory and grace

[www.ccli.com CCLI Song #15960 Words: Public Domain]

Nineteen

Heavenly Vision

*I love the house where you live, O Lord,
the place where your glory dwells.*
Psalm 26:8

On January 31, 2018, a celestial phenomenon occurred when the sun, earth, and moon aligned. There was a supermoon lunar eclipse. Depending upon their location, some people observed an immense orange moon hanging low in the sky.

Another heavenly wonder, Aurora Borealis, occurs in certain parts of the world. These northern lights appear when storms on the sun send gusts of particles hurtling through space. As they interact with atmospheric molecules, they form an aurora, a curtain of wavy green, pink, and white light.

Such spectacles cause people to look up. I wonder if the Lord creates these celestial events to remind us to look to Him. Living on the ground, we tend to have lateral vision because earthly concerns occupy our thoughts. Maybe these sky events are God's way of improving our heavenly vision.

The book of Revelation describes a city in heaven. "It shone with the glory of God, and its brilliance was like that of a very precious jewel, like a jasper, clear as crystal" (Revelation 21:11). "The great street of the city was of pure gold, like transparent glass" (Revelation 21:21). This description of a future heavenly home inspires us to focus on a place beyond earth and to look toward eternity.

Some people have keen heavenly vision. They regularly look to God for guidance and protection. Prayer is as natural to them as breathing. They speak with a wisdom that comes only from God.

These people aren't distracted by the cares of this world because they trust the Lord with every aspect of their lives.

I've known such people. They weren't perfect, but they inspired me to improve my heavenly vision.

Our lives change when we focus our eyes heavenward. The direction of our thinking changes so that we're less concerned about earthly matters and more concerned about spiritual matters. We ponder our purpose in the world. We become more mindful of our attitudes, our behaviors, and our use of time. We become more prayerful, laying every concern and request before God. We begin to rely on God in every circumstance because we trust Him more and more. Most importantly, we become more worshipful and thankful, continually praising God for His goodness. As you and I consistently focus our eyes on God, we improve our heavenly vision.

Lord, draw our attention upward so our eyes continually focus on You.

Personal Reflections

Discussion Questions

1. According to the hymn, what are the results of turning our eyes upon Jesus?

2. Would you rate your vision as more vertical or horizontal? Why? What must you do to increase your heavenly vision?

3. **Delve deeper:** Read Revelation 21. Which part of this heavenly vision excites you? Why?

My God The Spring Of All My Joys
Isaac Watts

My God the spring of all my joys
The life of my delights
The glory of my brightest days
And comfort of my night

In darkest shades if thou appear
My dawning is begun
Thou art my soul's bright morning star
And thou my rising sun

The opening heavens around me shine
With beams of sacred bliss
If Jesus shows His mercy mine
And whispers I am His

My soul would leave this heavy clay
At that transporting word
Run up with joy the shining way
To see and praise my Lord

Fearless of hell and ghastly death
I'd break through every foe
The wings of love and arms of faith
Would bear me conquer through

[www.ccli.com CCLI Song #7042426 Public Domain]

Twenty

Morning Star

*I am the Root and Offspring of David,
and the bright Morning Star.*
Revelation 22:16

At dawn, just before sunrise, while the sky still holds onto the last bit of darkness, one star gleams above the horizon. A single point of light penetrates the navy sky—the morning star.

In ancient times, the word star meant *point of light*. The point of light that shines in the morning sky is actually the planet Venus which the Greeks named "Phosphorus." It means *bringer of light*. How appropriate that Jesus refers to Himself as the Morning Star, a point of light, and a bringer of light.

The morning star appears when the sky is still dark. And so, Jesus, our morning star, makes His presence known when our lives seem most bleak. He's a point of light that penetrates our despair.

Several hymns have been written about the Morning Star. The lyrics speak of a bright star that draws us toward its source. They describe a hope that transports the hurting beyond their sorrows to a place of joy. Desperate people are drawn to a light of hope.

Leah, the first wife of Jacob, desperately sought a flicker of hope. She was unloved because Jacob loved her sister Rachel, his second wife. "When the Lord saw that Leah was not loved, he opened her womb, but Rachel was barren" (Genesis 29:31). God blessed Leah with fertility, and she birthed seven children. Her sons comprise most of the tribes of Israel.

God filled Leah's emptiness with a multitude of progeny. She may not have been loved by her husband, but she was abundantly blessed by God's love. King David descended from her bloodline, and through David's, came Jesus. The bright Morning Star came through Leah!

God sees our desperation, our sadness, our loneliness, and our pain. He doesn't leave us without hope. When we're distraught, the Lord shines light into our greatest fear, our deepest sadness, and our most complex problem. Jesus is a point of light that draws us toward hope. He glows with grace, mercy, and love.

With each trial we face, Jesus, our Morning Star, shines upon us. He sees our struggles. He knows our sadness. Jesus never leaves us in darkness. With a divine glow, He draws us to Himself.

Perhaps you're going through a difficult time and all seems dark. Perhaps you're desperately searching for a pinprick of light. The Morning Star shines for you. If you look to Jesus, He'll bring light and hope into your life.

Lord, thank you for being our Morning Star.
You are the point of light that shines with hope.
You are the Bringer of our Light.

Personal Reflections

Discussion Questions

1. How does the hymn describe the Lord?

2. Can you recall a time when Jesus brought light into a dark moment? Did He bring clarity, a new perspective, or hope? Explain.

3. **Delve deeper:** Read Genesis 28:10-22. How did the Lord bring light to Jacob? Has the Lord ever spoken to you in a dream?

Praise the Lord Ye Heavens Adore Him

Anonymous

Praise the Lord you heavens adore Him
Praise him angels in the height
Sun and moon rejoice before Him
Praise Him all ye stars of light

Praise the Lord for He has spoken
Worlds His mighty voice obeyed
Laws which never shall be broken
For their guidance has He made

Praise the Lord for He is glorious
Never shall His promise fail
God has made His saints victorious
Sin and death shall not prevail

Praise the God of our salvation
Hosts on high His pow'rs proclaim
Heav'n and earth and all creation
Laud and magnify His name

[www.ccli.com CCLI Song #2728313 Public Domain]

Twenty-one

In Praise of God

*Who is like the Lord our God, the One who sits
enthroned on high, who stoops down to look
on the heavens and the earth?*
Psalm 113:5-6

Tonight against a deep blue sky, heaven praised God with a billion twinkling lights. Sparkling diamonds amassed overhead as a testament of God's spectacular plan for the sky. The stars praised the Almighty with brilliant flickers.

God sits enthroned above heaven and earth, yet He has a master plan for everything He created. When God stoops to look upon heaven and earth, He sees His plan in progress.

For the first twenty years of my life, I rarely attended church. I never read the Bible. I knew only a few Bible stories from my occasional attendance in a Sunday school class. One summer, my Aunt Mary took me to her church's Vacation Bible School. That's when I asked Jesus to come into my heart. Beyond that experience, I grew up without religious training.

But God's plan for me was underway. I was twenty-one when He worked a major breakthrough in my life. My boyfriend and I had set out to hitchhike across country. At that time, hitchhikers were a common site along interstates. They held up cardboard signs touting a destination; ours said California. But the Lord met me in Nevada in a pup tent. One night while I was alone in the tent, God made His presence known to me. I was immediately aware of His holiness and my sinfulness. I cried, begging God to forgive me. He showered me with mercy and grace. My heart was changed forever. Each day, I praise God for continuing to work His wonderful plan in me.

Psalm 113 is about everyone and everything praising God for His perfect plan. The sun, the sky, and the stars participate in God's plan by being everything He designed them to be. The beauty they exhibit as they praise the Creator is astounding.

We weren't created to shine from the sky, but God has a remarkable plan for each one of us. God designed us to find fulfillment in Him alone. He created us to lean on Him when we need strength, to find comfort in Him when we hurt, to hide in Him when we're afraid, and to commune with Him throughout each day. We were designed to need God to satisfy our longings. And the best part of God's plan is that He sent His Son to redeem us.

We participate in God's plan by accepting Jesus as our Savior. We participate by depending on God for everything and by allowing Him to work in us and through us. Our participation is an act of praise.

The Lord's plan for us will be complete on the day we join the angels in heaven to sing praise to God forever. On that day, our praise will be astoundingly beautiful.

Father, we're humbled that You would desire
to work a perfect plan in us. May we praise Your name forever.

Personal Reflections

Discussion Questions

1. According to this hymn, who and what praise God? How do they show their praise?

2. For what do you continually praise God? Why?

3. **Delve deeper:** Read Psalm 113. Who should praise God? Why should we praise God? What can you do to improve in the area of praise?

Sweet Peace The Gift Of God's Love

Peter Philip Bilhorn

There comes to my heart one sweet strain
A glad and joyous refrain
I sing it again and again
Sweet peace the gift of God's love

Thro' Christ on the cross
Peace was made
My debt by His death
Was all paid
No other foundation is laid
For peace the gift of God's love

In Jesus for peace I abide
And as I keep close to His side
There's nothing but peace doth betide
Sweet peace the gift of God's love

Chorus:
Peace peace sweet peace
Wonderful gift from above
Oh wonderful wonderful peace
Sweet peace the gift of God's love

[www.ccli.com CCLI Song #122262 Public Domain]

Twenty-two

From Sunrise to Sunset

*I lie down and sleep; I wake again,
because the Lord sustains me.*

Psalm 3:5

Today I awoke to a sky draped with colorful sashes, as though Joseph's beautifully colored cloak, the one given to him by a father who loved him immensely, flounced above the horizon.

Israel, the father of Joseph, expressed his special love for his son by giving him a colorful cloak. It must have been exceptionally beautiful to be mentioned in the Bible. "Now Israel loved Joseph more than any of his other sons, because he had been born to him in his old age; and he made a richly ornamented robe for him" (Genesis 37:3).

The beauty of Joseph's robe symbolized a father's love, but it was love for only one son. Unfortunately, the robe stirred up jealousy in Joseph's brothers. Every day, from sunup to sundown, when they looked at Joseph, they were reminded of their father's special love for him.

Unlike Joseph's father, our Heavenly Father has a special love for *each* of us. No one is loved more than another. God's love is boundless and abundant. It overflows the sky in neon colors at sunup and sundown. The Father's intense passion streaks above our heads as a spectrum of light, an iridescent display to remind us we are loved beyond measure. The Lord pours out his love in the form of sky-gifts at sunrise and sunset. Each multicolored gift is a declaration of love from our Father. We can go to sleep each night knowing we're loved and cared for.

My granddaughter can't fall asleep without her favorite blanket. If it's missing from her bed, her parents have to search the house until they find it. Then with wiggles of delight, she grabs her "bankie" and turns it until she finds the corner with the loose thread. As she rubs the thread against her nose, she drifts into a peaceful sleep. Her blanket is her comfort and security.

Our sense of comfort and security comes from knowing that the One who wraps the sky in a prismatic blanket is the same One who loves us beyond measure. Our loving Father oversees all that concerns us. Each night we can drift into tranquil sleep knowing we're enveloped in God's loving care.

Just as my granddaughter snuggles into her blanket, we can snuggle into our Father's love. He is our soft place. The Lord's affection for us is so abundant it spills from heaven into the sky. We need only look up to know we are loved from sunrise to sunset.

Heavenly Father, thank you for using brilliant colors in the sky to remind us of Your special love.

Personal Reflections

Discussion Questions

1. According to this hymn, how does God demonstrate His love for us?

2. Have you felt unloved by significant people in your life? In what ways has God filled that hole in your heart?

3. **Delve deeper:** Read Genesis 37. How was Joseph's cloak both a blessing and a curse? Compare the love of Joseph's father to God's love for us. What can we learn about parental love from this devotion?

It Is Well With My Soul

Horatio Gates Spafford, Philip Paul Bliss

When peace like a river
Attendeth my way
When sorrows like sea billows roll
Whatever my lot
Thou hast taught me to say
It is well
It is well with my soul

My sin O the bliss
Of this glorious tho't
My sin not in part but the whole
Is nailed to the cross
And I bear it no more
Praise the Lord
Praise the Lord O my soul

And Lord haste the day
When the faith shall be sight
The clouds be rolled back as a scroll
The trump shall resound
And the Lord shall descend
Even so it is well
With my soul

Chorus:
It is well with my soul
It is well
It is well with my soul

[www.ccli.com CCLI Song #25376 Public Domain]

Twenty-three

Like a Weaned Child

But I have stilled and quieted my soul.
Psalm 131:2

The moon is a silver crescent gleaming overhead, and the evening sky wraps around me like a deep blue comforter. I'm the only one out walking in the still of the night.

A personal issue is making me anxious, so I decide to let my feet pound out my stress. As I stride down the sidewalk, a Bible verse comes to mind. "My heart is not proud, O Lord, my eyes are not haughty; I do not concern myself with great matters or things too wonderful for me" (Psalm 131:1). Those words stop me. I suddenly realize that the matter upsetting me is too great for me to handle on my own. There are things I can't understand because I'm not God.

Admitting my helplessness frees me from having to solve my problem. My tension eases, and as I turn my thoughts to God's majesty, a sense of peace washes over me.

The Lord makes a way for us to have peace in our hearts. If we think about His magnificence instead of our problems, a calmness, as soothing as gentle moonlight, settles over our spirits.

Even David, a mighty warrior and powerful king, turned his thoughts to God when troubles overwhelmed him. He compared the experience to being like a weaned child with his mother. "Like a weaned child is my soul within me" (Psalm 131:2).

A weaned child differs from a nursing child who squirms and cries until his mother suckles him at her breast. A weaned child enjoys the simple pleasure of being close to Mama. As she strokes his sweaty brow and hums a lullaby, the child relaxes, inhaling her familiar scent and listening to the soft sound of her voice. He's perfectly at peace beside his mother.

That's the picture David paints for us in Psalm 131— the picture of a still and quiet child. When we give our worries to the Lord, we're like a child sitting beside Mama. The Lord strokes our sweaty brows and softly sings over us. As we lean into His tenderness, His voice stills and quiets us. Our bodies go limp as our tension dissipates.

The Lord wants us to live with peace in our hearts and to not fret over matters that are too great for us. He will take care of the things that worry us. We can be like a weaned child at perfect rest beside our Heavenly Father.

Being still beside the Lord is like being draped with moonlight and wrapped in deep blue comfort.

Father, keep us in the quiet stillness of Your presence.

Personal Reflections

Discussion Questions

1. According to the hymn, why can we say all is well with our souls?

2. Can you recall a time, as either a child or an adult, when you felt the way David describes as being still and quiet like a weaned child? How did that moment impact your spirit? Your spiritual life?

3. **Delve deeper:** Read Psalm 131. Discuss how each verse impacts you. What new understanding have you gained from the message in this short psalm?

Quiet Moments in Nature, Lessons from the Sky

Amazing Grace

John Newton

Amazing grace how sweet the sound
That saved a wretch like me
I once was lost but now am found
Was blind but now I see

'Twas grace that taught my heart to fear
And grace my fears relieved
How precious did that grace appear
The hour I first believed

Through many dangers toils and snares
I have already come
'Tis grace that brought me safe thus far
And grace will lead me home

When we've been there ten thousand years
Bright shining as the sun
We've no less days to sing God's praise
Than when we've first begun

[www.ccli.com CCLI Song #4755360 Words: Public Domain]

Twenty-four

The Sound of Grace

*In him we have redemption through his blood,
the forgiveness of sins, in accordance with the riches
of God's grace that he lavished on us
with all wisdom and understanding.*
Ephesians 1:7-8

A lone bagpiper stood on a cliff to serenade the sunset. Musical notes floated through the air and into my ears. The song he played was *Amazing Grace*. As I hummed along, two questions came to my mind: *What is sound? What is the sound of grace?*

An internet search explained that sound is the result of pressure waves emanating from a vibrating object. They compress and stretch as they move through air, water, or a solid medium to our ears. The condition of our ears determines our ability to hear the sound waves.

The sound of grace, however, must be explained with real life examples. I heard the sound of grace after God shook my foundations with a supersonic boom. The moment God opened my eyes to see my sins, my world seemed to shake and rumble. Guilt thundered in my heart. But the noise lasted only a second because the Lord silenced it with a whisper of grace.

He reached out to me, lifted my chin, and wiped my tears with His thumbs. As I dared to raise my eyes, the Lord smiled and whispered, *You're forgiven*. Sound waves of amazing grace reverberated in my soul. It was the sweetest sound I'd ever heard.

God sends sound waves of grace into our souls when we come to Him desperate for forgiveness and mercy. Even though we may first hear a thunderclap of guilt, it's immediately followed by a gentle melody of grace.

There's no reason we should fear the revelation of our sins; Jesus already paid the penalty we deserve. But we need to admit and repent of our sins so we truly comprehend the depth and breadth of God's grace. Once we're aware of our sinful condition, our hearts become receptive so we're able to hear the sound waves of grace that emanate from the Lord.

A vivid example of the sound of grace is found in Luke 7:36-38. A woman who had earlier trembled at the boom of her guilt, received grace from Jesus. Later, during a dinner party, she approached Jesus. Kneeling before the Lord, she kissed His feet, washed them with her tears, and wiped them with her hair. The sound of grace so overwhelmed her heart that it flowed out of her in the form of tears.

The Lord's sweet grace is available to all who will receive it. Have you heard the sound of grace? It's an amazing sound.

Lord, we're desperate for Your grace.

Personal Reflections

Discussion Questions

1. Name some of the aspects of grace mentioned in this hymn.

2. Can you recall a time when you offered grace to another person? Have you received grace from another person? Describe the emotions you felt with each example.

3. **Delve deeper:** Read Luke 7:36-50. In what ways does Jesus offer grace to others? Whose ears heard the sound of grace most clearly? Why?

To God Be The Glory

Fanny Jane Crosby, William Howard Doane

To God be the glory great things He has done
So loved He the world that He gave us His Son
Who yielded His life an atonement for sin
And opened the life gate that all may go in

O perfect redemption the purchase of blood
To every believer the promise of God
The vilest offender who truly believes
That moment from Jesus a pardon receives

Great things He has taught us
Great things He has done
And great our rejoicing through Jesus the Son
But purer and higher and greater will be
Our wonder our transport when Jesus we see

Chorus:
Praise the Lord praise the Lord
Let the earth hear His voice
Praise the Lord praise the Lord
Let the people rejoice
O Come to the Father through Jesus the Son
And give Him the glory great things He has done

[www.ccli.com CCLI Song #23426 Public Domain]

Twenty-five

Invisible and Visible

*He is the image of the invisible God,
the firstborn over all creation.*
Colossians 1:15

In the far reaches of outer space, an invisible line known as the Karman Line, encircles the earth. It's an imaginary marker defining the edge of outer space. Theodore von Karman set this line in 1957. Since it's invisible, the only way to *see* it is to measure up a hundred kilometers from sea level. The Karman line regulates international space travel by designating any area beyond the Karman Line as open for exploration.

God, the Creator of outer space, is invisible to us, yet He gives us a way to *see* Him. He reveals all of His qualities in the human form of Jesus. We can see God by looking at Jesus.

People have various concepts of who the invisible God is. Some people refer to Him as *the man upstairs.* Others consider God to be far removed from life on earth. They think of Him as a being who watches from a distance but doesn't involve Himself in day-to-day happenings. Some people see God as a severe judge whose purpose is to dispense punishment. But God clears up these misconceptions by revealing Himself in the bodily form of Jesus Christ. "For God was pleased to have all his fullness dwell in him, and through him to reconcile to himself all things, whether things on earth or things in heaven, by making peace through his blood, shed on the cross" (Colossians 1:19-20).

The invisible God placed all of His fullness into the human form of Jesus Christ, and through Jesus, He reconciles sinners to Himself.

In the Old Testament, people were grateful to have an invisible God because they believed that anyone who saw God's face would die. We may not be able to see God's face, but we can look at His heart—it's revealed in the body of Jesus.

In Jesus, we see evidence of God's incredible love for us. The visible man who hung on the cross was the embodiment of the invisible God sacrificing Himself for us. God's fullness was in the crucified human body of Jesus. No one loves and cherishes us more than God in the living form of Jesus. Our invisible Father visibly gave all of Himself for us.

*Holy Savior and God, we stand amazed in Your presence.
Thank you for making Yourself visible to us.*

Personal Reflections

Discussion Questions

1. This hymn declares that all glory belongs to God. Why is that true?

2. Jesus is the visible image of God. Does that fact influence your understanding of God? How?

3. **Delve deeper:** Read 1 John 1:1; John 6:35, 8:12, 10:9, 14:6. Have you ever thought about these attributes of God? How do they impact you personally?

Near To The Heart of God

Cleland Boyd McAfee

There is a place of quiet rest
Near to the heart of God
A place where sin cannot molest
Near to the heart of God

There is a place of comfort sweet
Near to the heart of God
A place where we our Savior meet
Near to the heart of God

There is a place of full release
Near to the heart of God
A place where all is joy and peace
Near to the heart of God

Chorus:
O Jesus blest Redeemer
Sent from the heart of God
Hold us who wait before thee
Near to the heart of God

[www.ccli.com CCLI Song #93700 Words: Public Domain]

Twenty-six

A Place of Cool Refreshment

*Though I walk in the midst of trouble,
you preserve my life.*
Psalm 138:7

A cool breeze floats across my cheeks and arms during my early morning walk. I like this time of day because the temperature is refreshing. Later, the summer sun will ignite the air with heat.

Morning is also the time of day I sit quietly with the Lord. He refreshes my spirit before I face the heat of daily challenges.

Just as summer days can become uncomfortably hot, so can troubles when they bear down on us. They deplete our energy so we feel weak and worn out. But in the Lord's presence, there's a place of morning coolness, a place of refreshment and renewal.

David knew about this place. In Psalm 138, he writes of finding relief near the Lord. David's refreshment came from knowing God was beside him, helping him during the heat of trials.

The Lord invites each of us to enter a place where we can find relief from our troubles. That place is in His presence.

As surely as summer brings its share of heat, each day brings its share of challenges. We can't avoid troubles; however, when they press upon us, the Lord invites us into the cool of His presence. As we sit a spell in God's air conditioning, we're revived.

The Lord refreshes us in various ways. Through the beauty of nature, He lifts our spirits. We can feel His hug in gentle breezes. His sweet essence wafts from nearby flowers to delight our senses. Each nature gift is a reminder that God is near.

The Lord also refreshes us as we pray. Talking with God forges a spiritual connection that renews our spirit. As we bow in prayer, we remember that the recipient of our prayers has power to help us. Jesus sought out solitary places where He spent hours in prayer. He needed the Father to revitalize Him so He could resume His mission.

The Bible is another place where we can find refreshment. It contains messages of encouragement and hope. As we read divinely inspired words, we're energized by God's promises. The Lord assures us He'll never fail us.

Has the heat of a personal problem left you wilted or exhausted? Are you depleted of energy and hope? There is a place of refreshment available to you. You'll find it when you move closer to God.

The Lord revives us and gives us strength to endure every trial. When we feel worn out by life's troubles, God invites us to enter the refreshing coolness of His presence.

Lord, we seek You in our time of need. Thank you for being like an early morning breeze that revives our spirits.

Personal Reflections

Discussion Questions

1. How does this hymn depict the place that's near to God's heart?

2. Think about the hottest summer day you've experienced. How did you find refreshment from the heat? Compare that to the way God has refreshed you during your trials.

3. **Delve deeper:** Read Psalm 138. How does David respond to the refreshment that comes from God? In what ways did God refresh David during his time of trial?

At Thy Feet Our God And Father

James D. Burns

At your feet our God and Father
Who has blessed us all our days
We with grateful hearts now gather
To begin the day with praise

Praise for light so brightly shining
On our steps from heaven above
Praise for mercies daily twining
Round us golden cords of love

Jesus for your love most tender
On the cross for sinners shown
We would praise you and surrender
All our hearts to be your own

Every day will be the brighter
As your gracious face we view
Every burden will be lighter
If we bear it Lord with you

Spread your love's bright banner o'er us
Give us strength to serve and wait
Till the glory breaks before us
Through the city's open gate

[www.ccli.com CCLI Song #3329924 Public Domain]

Twenty-seven

Transforming Light

The people walking in darkness have seen a great light.
Isaiah 9:2

The sky was dismal, shrouded with gray clouds. Suddenly, sunlight pierced the clouds and unfurled shafts of golden sunbeams. An ethereal fan of light transformed the dreary sky into a luminous vista.

The light of God's Son transforms our lives from gray to glorious. Jesus came to earth for that very purpose. Prophets of the Old Testament foretold of one who would bring spiritual enlightenment and hope to mankind.

Not only does Jesus shine into our spiritual darkness, He also shines into our personal darkness. He's able to pierce shadows of sadness or depression with golden shafts of hope.

Throughout my years as a Christian, Jesus repeatedly infused my gray days with light and hope. Yes, Christians have dark times. Some people think that believers live untroubled lives, but that's not the case. We suffer the pain of this world. Our hearts get broken. We experience disappointments, emotional trauma, and losses. Our lives are not picture perfect unless it's a picture of storms.

Why shouldn't we experience dark times? Jesus did. He knew the lure of temptation. He suffered hardship, heartache, and agonizing physical pain. The Lord didn't live on earth without experiencing trouble. He struggled in the same ways that we do. But Jesus suffered for our benefit so that He would be a merciful and compassionate Savior. "For we do not have a high priest who is unable to sympathize with our weaknesses, but we have one who has been tempted in every way, just as we are—yet was without sin" (Hebrews 4:15).

Jesus understands how we feel. When we take our sadness, depression, temptation, and pain to Him, He offers us compassion. We can share every heartache with the One who suffered the same heartaches we experience.

Whether our trials last for a time period or for a lifetime, we don't have to feel disheartened. When Jesus gets involved, transformation takes place. He said, "I am the light of the world. Whoever follows me will never walk in darkness, but will have the light of life" (John 8:12).

Is a dark cloud hovering over you? Call out to Jesus. He brightens our lonely moments with His companionship. He holds us close when we need a shoulder for our tears. He gives us strength to withstand temptation. He soothes our pain with His healing touch. When we rely on Jesus, He transforms our darkest times into moments filled with His resplendent light.

Lord, we need Your light in our lives.

Personal Reflections

Discussion Questions

1. The hymn states that the light of God transforms our lives? How?

2. Can you recall a dark time that was transformed by the Lord's light and love? Explain.

3. **Delve deeper:** Read Isaiah 53. Why do you think Jesus is able to help us during our times of darkness? Which verse has special meaning to you? Why?

Does Jesus Care
Frank E. Graeff

Does Jesus care when my heart is pained
Too deeply for mirth and song
As the burdens press and the cares distress
And the way grows weary and long

Does Jesus care when my way is dark
With a nameless dread and fear
As the daylight fades into deep night shades
Does He care enough to be near

Does Jesus care when I've tried and failed
To resist some temptation strong
When for my deep grief I find no relief
Though my tears flow all the night long

Does Jesus care when I've said goodbye
To the dearest on earth to me
And my sad heart aches till it nearly breaks
Is it aught to Him does He see

Chorus:
O yes He cares I know He cares
His heart is touched with my grief
When the days are weary
The long nights dreary
I know my Savior cares

[www.ccli.com CCLI Song #3253100 Public Domain]

Twenty-eight

Unpredictable

O Lord, you have seen this; be not silent.
Psalm 35:22

March weather is unpredictable in Florida. One day humid air lays over everything like a moist blanket. The next day winds wail, hurtling rain sideways against windows. Upper air currents pound their feet in the clouds and raise a victory arm that crackles with electricity. Then on other days, March churns up wind gusts that swirl and laugh with delight.

Life can be as unpredictable as March. One day circumstances fall upon us like humid air from which there seems no relief. But during those times, we can find comfort beneath the shade-prayers of friends. Their prayers help us remember that God hears us when we call out to Him. Their prayers remind us that God sees our troubles and He won't be silent.

Friends of the Apostle Peter prayed fervently when he was unjustly imprisoned. Their prayers were like a delightful breeze refreshing Peter. God heard each prayer and was not silent. During the night, He sent an angel to rescue Peter. The outcome of Peter's situation may have been unpredictable, but God's help was certain.

Sometimes trouble thunders in like a March storm, and we're deluged with trials. I know a family who faced such a time. Their eight-year-old daughter was diagnosed with cancer, the C word that stabs the heart like a bolt of lightning. Who can withstand the shock? The family and the church cried out to God. They lifted desperate hands to heaven, asking God to see their troubles and not be silent.

Their violent storm lasted for months. The parents held vigil at the hospital while friends and family helped to care for the siblings. It was a time of unceasing prayer, tears, and fears. But the Lord was gracious. God saw, and He helped. The day came when a cancer-free child stood between two grateful parents at the front of the church. Everyone praised God. The cancer-free diagnosis swirled through the church bringing gusts of joy.

You may be experiencing a trial that blustered into your life unexpectedly. It may be hurtling challenges at you that make your heart pound with fear. You don't need to face those challenges alone. Reach out to people who will offer shade-prayers on your behalf. Lean on people who will support you when you can't stand on your own. But most importantly, know that you can count on the Lord. He is always predictable.

We can be certain that God will always help us. The Lord sees and knows our suffering: He won't be silent. "The Lord be exalted, who delights in the well-being of his servant" (Psalm 35:27). Yes, He always cares.

Father, thank you for always seeing, knowing, and helping us.

Personal Reflections

Discussion Questions

1. The hymn states that Jesus cares about our struggles. What struggles are mentioned?

2. Sometimes we're able to see and know what someone is going through without them telling us. Why do you think that's possible? What does that tell us about God's ability to see and know what we go through?

3. **Delve deeper:** Read Psalm 35:17-28. How does David deal with the unpredictable trials of his life?

Whiter Than Snow

James Nicholson

Lord Jesus I long to be perfectly whole
I want Thee forever to live in my soul
Break down ev'ry idol cast out ev'ry foe
Now wash me and I shall be whiter than snow

Lord Jesus look down from Thy throne in the skies
And help me to make a complete sacrifice
I give up myself and whatever I know
Now wash me and I shall be whiter than snow

Lord Jesus for this I most humbly entreat
I wait blessed Lord at Thy crucified feet
By faith for my cleansing I see Thy blood flow
Now wash me and I shall be whiter than snow

Lord Jesus Thou seest I patiently wait
Come now and within me a new heart create
To those who have sought Thee Thou never saidst no
Now wash me and I shall be whiter than snow

The blessing by faith I receive from above
O glory my soul is made perfect in love
My prayer has prevailed and this moment I know
The blood is applied I am whiter than snow

Chorus:
(1) Whiter than snow yes whiter than snow
Now wash me and I shall be whiter than snow

(2) Whiter than snow yes whiter than snow
The blood is applied I am whiter than snow

[www.ccli.com CCLI Song #3110401 Public Domain]

Twenty-nine

Snowy Whiteness

*Cleanse me with hyssop and I will be clean;
wash me and I will be whiter than snow.*
Psalm 51:7

In the silence of night, snowflakes fluttered from the dark sky and covered the ground. I awoke to a pristine landscape, a field of glistening ice crystals. Beneath this glacial blanket, the ground was a vision of snowy whiteness.

Snow covers every trace of dirt. After a snowstorm, no matter how much debris is scattered about, the land looks perfectly clean. Snow has the ability to make the dirtiest ground white.

Jesus is the embodiment of snowy whiteness. He's the only one who ever lived without being soiled by the muck of sin. We, on the other hand, are like a muddy riverbank. There's nothing we can do to make ourselves clean.

But our situation isn't hopeless. If snow can make the worst patch of ground look like a field of sparkling crystals, Jesus can do even more for us. He can make us as white as snow.

The Bible gives examples of people who were cleansed by the Lord. The woman who was caught in adultery was offered the opportunity to become clean. Instead of condemning her for her sin, Jesus said, "Go now and leave your life of sin" (John 8:11).

The thief on the cross next to Jesus repented of the sins that put him there. When he asked Jesus for mercy, he received a promise of eternal life with the Lord.

Even the mob who clamored for Jesus to be crucified received cleansing when they were "cut to the heart." They asked the apostles, "'Brothers, what shall we do?' Peter replied, 'Repent and be baptized, every one of you, in the name of Jesus Christ for the forgiveness of your sins'" (Acts 2:37-38).

If people who seemed hopelessly soiled could be cleansed by Jesus, we can too. He can wash away our dirt and make us as pure as freshly fallen snow.

In Psalm 51, David asked the Lord to wash him and make him whiter than snow. David had committed terrible sins that hurt others. When his sins were exposed, he cried out to God for mercy. He knew his cleansing could only come from God.

Our cleansing is possible only through the sacrifice of Jesus. He bore our transgressions on the cross so we could live a new life and be free of our past sins. The Lord can wash away every trace of dirt from our souls. When we approach God with repentant hearts, He replies, "Though your sins are like scarlet, they shall be as white as snow" (Isaiah 1:18). The Lord can make us pristine.

Oh, Lord, we come to you for soul cleansing.
Cover our sins with snowy whiteness.

Personal Reflections

Discussion Questions

1. The hymn describes the reasons and benefits of being washed by the Lord. What are they?

2. Have you experienced soul cleansing? When? How did it make you feel? Do you think our souls can be cleansed more than once? Explain.

3. **Delve deeper:** Read Psalm 51. Describe David's experience of soul cleansing. How does his experience apply to our lives?

Softly Now The Light Of Day

Carl Maria von Weber, George Washington Doane

Softly now the light of day
Fades upon our sight away
Free from care from labor free
Lord we would commune with Thee

Thou whose all pervading eye
Nought escapes without within
Pardon each infirmity
Open fault and secret sin

Soon from us the light of day
Shall forever pass away
Then from sin and sorrow free
Take us Lord to dwell with Thee

Thou who sinless yet hast known
All of man's infirmity
Then from Thine eternal throne
Jesus look with pitying eye

Ending:
Amen

[www.ccli.com CCLI Song #752993]

Thirty

Sunset Reflections

*For as high as the heavens are above the earth,
so great is his love for those who fear him.*
Psalm 103:11

Bold colors streak the sky then gradually mellow to pastels as the sun sets. I sit outside enjoying the sun's final descent; an aura of peacefulness surrounds me.

Sunset is a time to slow down and reflect upon the day while nature prepares everything for night. It's a time to give thanks to God for the blessings He sprinkled over us all day.

In the beginning verses of Psalm 103, we read David's words of thanks, "Praise the Lord, O my soul; all my inmost being, praise his holy name. Praise the Lord, O my soul, and forget not all his benefits—who forgives all your sins." I wonder if David composed those words at sunset.

In this beautiful psalm, David wrote about all that God had done for him. He thanked God for forgiveness of sins, for healing from diseases, for redemption, compassion, and justice. He recalled how the Lord satisfied his desires with good things. David counted his blessings.

Counting our blessings is the perfect way to end each day. It puts our minds into a state of contentment. It helps us move into alignment with the Lord as we acknowledge Him as the giver and us as receivers. Sunset provides a beautiful setting for us to reflect upon God's goodness and to give thanks for His blessings.

Reflection, though, isn't always a pleasant experience. If we look back over a day filled with mistakes and regrets, we may prefer to forget. But the Lord accommodates those times too.

"As a father has compassion on his children, so the Lord has compassion on those who fear him; for he knows how we are formed, he remembers that we are dust" (Psalm 103:13). God knows our limitations. He doesn't expect us to be perfect. When we confess our wrongs, the Lord blesses us with unlimited forgiveness and grace.

We show reverence and holy fear when we ask forgiveness from the Most High and Holy One. God shows compassion to us when He bestows grace and mercy upon us. "He does not treat us as our sins deserve or repay us according to our iniquities" (Psalm 103:10). "As far as the east is from the west, so far has he removed our transgressions from us" (Psalm 103:12).

A sunset sky is a glorious reminder of the immensity of God's mercy. The next time we gaze upon a setting sun, we can reflect upon God's holiness. We can recall our blessings and confess our sins. We can thank the Lord for His sky-sized grace. Sunset is the perfect time for reflection.

Lord, as we marvel at the beauty of sunset,
we meditate on Your goodness.

Personal Reflections

Doris Hoover

Discussion Questions

1. According to the hymn, what happens between us and God at sunset?

2. Do you consider a time of reflection to be pleasant or unpleasant? Why do you think that is?

3. **Delve deeper:** Read Psalm 103. Which of God's blessings are most meaningful to you at this moment in time? Explain.

There Is A Name I Love To Hear (There Is A Name)

Frederick Whitfield, Anonymous

There is a name I love to hear
I love to sing its worth
It sounds like music in my ear
The sweetest name on earth

It tells me of a Savior's love
Who died to set me free
It tells me of his precious blood
The sinner's perfect plea

It tells of one whose loving heart
Can feel my deepest woe
Who in each sorrow bears a part
That none can bear below

Chorus:
O how I love Jesus
O how I love Jesus
O how I love Jesus
Because he first loved me

[www.ccli.com CCLI Song #28696 Public Domain]

Thirty-one

My Story

Many, O Lord my God, are the wonders you have done.
Psalm 40:5

Today's temperature is delightfully refreshing. It's a perfect day for a walk. As I start down the recreation trail, sunbeams hitch a ride on my shoulders. Above me clouds stretch like lacey ribbons across a blue gabardine sky. I walk past a bed of purple and yellow pansies that glisten with droplets of dew, and a sweet fragrance rises to meet me. It's a lovely spring day.

In nature, spring only comes after the harsh conditions of winter pass. Life can be like that also. Sometimes we have to get through winter trials before entering a season filled with spring joy.

The winter season of my life is behind me as I step onto the threshold of spring. My trials have passed. I envision the beginning of this new season as a gate to a meadow of daisies, my favorite flowers. Yet I hesitate to step through the gate. I'm reluctant to embrace the joy that awaits me because I'm afraid I'll lose the intimacy I shared with the Lord during my winter trials. I'm afraid that stepping into joy means stepping away from my closeness to the Lord.

Eventually, I allow myself to take a tentative step through the imaginary gate. As I stand on the edge of a dream field of daisies, Jesus greets me. He grabs my hand and off we go, leaping and twirling across the grass, laughing until we fall on the ground breathless. Jesus points up to the sky, and I see them—dream clouds. Each cloud forms an image of one of my dreams. Then Jesus whispers, *They're all for you.*

Leaning against my best friend, I realize the closeness we shared during my season of winter trials is still here in my season of spring. The Lord's presence is steadfast. He'll never move away from me.

Intimacy with the Lord doesn't diminish when circumstances change. It lies behind us as cherished memories of God's ever-present help during our trials. But when our struggles pass, the Lord remains close beside us.

When we enter a season of joy, Jesus is there to twirl us and laugh with us. He loves to see our smiles. The Lord wants us to embrace our springtime wholeheartedly, without any hesitation.

Jesus is a friend who holds us during our sad times and dances with us during our happy times. He's the comfort in our winters and the joy in our springs.

Lord, we desire to be close to You in every season.
We rejoice in the wonders You work in our lives.

Personal Reflections

Discussion Questions

1. The author of the hymn gives his reasons for loving Jesus. What are they?

2. After a season of trials, have you ever hesitated to move forward and embrace a season of joy? Explain.

3. **Delve deeper:** Read Psalm 40. How does David act after going through a season of trials? In what ways are you inspired by his actions?

Made in United States
Orlando, FL
01 December 2022